Hippocrene
CHILDREN'S
ILLUSTRATED
JAPANESE
DICTIONARY

ENGLISH · JAPANESE
JAPANESE · ENGLISH

Compiled and translated by the Editors of Hippocrene Books

Interior illustrations by S. Grant (24, 81, 88); J. Gress (page 10, 21, 24, 37, 46, 54, 59, 65, 72, 75, 77); K. Migliorelli (page 13, 14, 18, 19, 20, 21, 22, 25, 31, 32, 37, 39, 40, 46, 47, 66, 71, 75, 76, 82, 86, 87); B. Swidzinska (page 9, 11, 12, 13, 14, 16, 23, 27, 28, 30, 32, 33, 35, 37, 38, 41, 42, 45, 46, 47, 48, 49, 50, 52, 53, 56, 57, 58, 59, 60, 61, 62, 63, 66, 68, 69, 70, 71, 72, 73, 75, 77, 78, 79, 83), N. Zhukov (page 8, 13, 14, 17, 18, 23, 27, 29, 33, 34, 39, 40, 41, 52, 64, 65, 71, 72, 73, 78, 84, 86, 88).

Design, prepress, and production: Graafiset International, Inc.

Cataloging-in-Publication Data available from the Library of Congress.

ISBN 0-7818-0817-0 (Hardcover edition)
ISBN 0-7818-0849-9 (Paperback edition)

Printed in Hong Kong.

For information, address:
Hippocrene Books, Inc.
171 Madison Avenue
New York, NY 10016

INTRODUCTION

With their absorbent minds, infinite curiosities and excellent memories, children have enormous capacities to master many languages. All they need is exposure and encouragement.

The easiest way to learn a foreign language is to simulate the same natural method by which a child learns English. The natural technique is built on the concept that language is representational of concrete objects and ideas. The use of pictures and words are the natural way for children to begin to acquire a new language.

The concept of this Illustrated Dictionary is to allow children to build vocabulary and initial competency naturally. Looking at the pictorial content of the Dictionary and saying and matching the words in connection to the drawings gives children the opportunity to discover the foreign language and thus, a new way to communicate.

The drawings in the Dictionary are designed to capture children's imaginations and make the learning process interesting and entertaining, as children return to a word and picture repeatedly until they begin to recognize it.

The beautiful images and clear presentation make this dictionary a wonderful tool for unlocking your child's multilingual potential.

Deborah Dumont, M.A., M.Ed.,
Child Psychologist and Educational Consultant

Japanese writing and pronunciation

The Japanese system of writing is very complicated and difficult to learn. It actually consists of three systems of signs used concurrently in most texts. The first, kanji, or Chinese characters, was borrowed from China and consists of ideograms (or hieroglyphics) representing the meaning of a word. There are more than two thousand characters used now in Japanese texts. Children's books usually contain a very limited number of characters (or do not contain any), and we do not use them in this Dictionary.

Japanese invented two syllabaries based graphically on Chinese characters. Each of them consists of 50 letters. *Katakana*, which is more simple to write and which is more angular, is used now for writing borrowed Western words. *Hiragana* is used for native Japanese words and Chinese borrowings.

HIRAGANA

あ a	か ka	さ sa	た ta	な na	は ha	ま ma	や ya	ら ra	わ wa
い i	き ki	し shi	ち chi	に ni	ひ hi	み mi		り ri	
う u	く ku	す su	つ tsu	ぬ nu	ふ hu	む mu	ゆ yu	る ru	
え e	け ke	せ se	て te	ね ne	へ he	め me		れ re	
お o	こ ko	そ so	と to	の no	ほ ho	も mo	よ yo	ろ ro	を wo
ん n									

KATAKANA

ア a	カ ka	サ sa	タ ta	ナ na	ハ ha	マ ma	ヤ ya	ラ ra	ワ wa
イ i	キ ki	シ shi	シ chi	ニ ni	ヒ hi	ミ mi		リ ri	
ウ u	ク ku	ス su	ツ tsu	ヌ nu	フ hu	ム mu	ユ yu	ル ru	
エ e	ケ ke	セ se	テ te	ネ ne	ヘ he	メ me		レ re	
オ o	コ ko	ソ so	ト to	ノ no	ホ ho	モ mo	ヨ yo	ロ ro	ヲ wo
ン n									

Japanese Pronunciation

Transliteration	Approximate English equivalent:
a	'a' in 'father'
i	'i' in 'machine'
u	'u' in 'put'
e	'e' in 'egg'
o	'o' in 'horse'
k before a,u,e,o	'c' in 'cool'
k before i, and ky	'c' in 'cute'
s before a,u,e,o	's' in 'see'
sh before i and shy	between 'sh' in 'she' and 's' in 'see'
t before a,e,o	't' in 'tip'
t turns 'ch' before i and chy	between 'ch' in 'cheap' and 't' in 'tip'
t turns 'ts' before u	'ts' in 'tsetse fly'
n before a, u, e, o	'n' in 'deny'
n before i and ny	'n' in 'menu' or 'avenue'
h before a, e, o	'h' in 'hot'
h before i and hy	'h' in 'humid'
m before a, u, e, o	'm' in 'remind'
m before i and my	'm' in 'amuse'
r before a,u,e,o	'r' in 'very'
z	'dz' in 'old zebra'

Japanese letters 'ki', 'shi', 'chi', 'ni', 'ri' with small letters 'ya', 'yu' and 'yo' behind them (きゃ,きゅ,きょ) indicate palatalized consonants and should read 'kya', 'kyu', 'kyo' and so on.

Two small parallel strokes at the upper right side of letters in rows 'k', 's', 't', 'h' (ガ,ギ,グ,ゲ,ゴ) indicate their full-voiced correspondences: 'g', 'z', 'd', 'b'.

A small round sign at the upper right corner of letters in a 'h' row (パ,ピ,プ) indicates that these syllables should begin with 'p'.

The letter 'u' (う) after syllabema ending with 'o' or 'u' indicates that this is a long vowel. For example, そ and う reads 'sō'. Macron sign shows the length of the vowel.

The small letter 'tsu' (っ,ッ) indicates that the following consonant should be doubled, for example, ざっし zasshi (magazine).

The letter 'wo' (を), which reads like 'o', in contemporary language serves only to indicate that the preceding word is the direct object of the verb.

airplane ひこうき
hikōki

alligator わに
wani

alphabet アルファベット
arufabetto

antelope かもしか
kamoshika

antlers しかのつの
shika-no tsuno

apple　リンゴ
ringo

aquarium　すいそう
suisō

arch　アーチ
āchi

arrow　や
ya

autumn　あき
aki

baby   あかちゃん
aka-chan

backpack   リュックサック
ryukkusakku

badger   たぬき
tanuki

baker   ぱんや
panya

ball   ボール
bōru

balloon   ふうせん
Hūsen

banana　バナナ
banana

barley　おおむぎ
ōmugi

barrel　たる
taru

basket　かご
kago

bat　こうもり
kōmori

beach　すなはま
sunahama

bear くま
kuma

beaver ビーバー
bībā

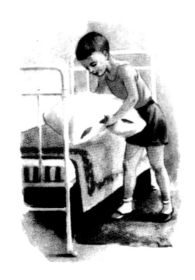

bed ベッド
beddo

bee はち
hachi

beetle かぶとむし
kabutomushi

bell ベル
beru

belt ベルト
beruto

bench ベンチ
benchi

bicycle じてんしゃ
jitensha

binoculars そうがんきょう
sōgankyō

bird とり
tori

birdcage とりかご
torikago

black くろ
kuro

blocks つみき
tsumiki

blossom はな
hana

blue あお
ao

boat ボート
bōto

bone ほね
hone

book　ほん
hon

boot　ブーツ
būtsu

bottle　びん
bin

bowl　どんぶり
donburi

boy　おとこのこ
otoko-noko

bracelet　ブレスレット
buresuretto

branch えだ
eda

bread パン
pan

breakfast あさごはん
asagohan

bridge はし
hashi

broom ほうき
hōki

brother あに、おとうと
ani, otōto

brown   ちゃいろ
chairo

brush   ブラシ
burashi

bucket   バケツ
baketsu

bulletin board   けいじばん
keijiban

bumblebee   マルハナバチ
maruhanabachi

butterfly   ちょう
chō

cab タクシー
takushī

cabbage キャベツ
kyabetsu

cactus サボテン
saboten

café きっさてん
kissaten

cake ケーキ
kēki

camel らくだ
rakuda

camera

カメラ
kamera

candle

ろうそく
rōsoku

candy

あめ
ame

canoe

カヌー
kanū

cap

キャップ
kyappu

captain

キャプテン、せんちょう
kyaputen, senchō

car　　　じどうしゃ
jidōsha

card　　　トランプ
toranpu

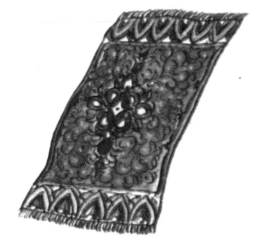

carpet　　カーペット、じゅうたん
kāpetto, jūtan

carrot　　　にんじん
ninjin

(to) carry　　はこぶ
hakobu

castle　　　しろ
shiro

cat ねこ
neko

cave ほらあな
hora ana

chair いす
isu

cheese チーズ
chīzu

cherry さくらんぼ
sakuranbo

chimney えんとつ
entotsu

chocolate　チョコレート
chokorēto

Christmas tree　クリスマスツリー
kurisumasu tsurī

circus　サーカス
sākasu

(to) climb　のぼる
noboru

cloud　くも
kumo

clown　どうけし
dōkeshi

coach ばしゃ
basha

coat コート
kōto

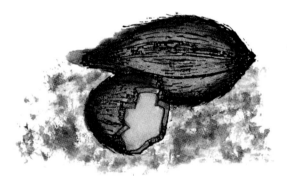

coconut ヤシのみ
yashi-no mi

comb くし
kushi

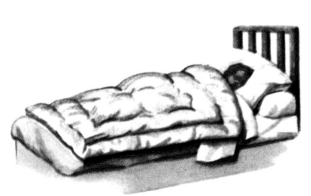

comforter ふとん
huton

compass らしんばん
rashinban

(to) cook　りょうりする
ryōri-suru

cork　コルク
koruku

corn　とうもろこし
tōmorokoshi

cow　めうし
meushi

cracker　クラッカー
kurakkā

cradle　ゆりかご
yurikago

(to) crawl　　　はう
hau

(to) cross　　　よこぎる
yokogiru

crown　　　かんむり
kanmuri

(to) cry　　　なく
naku

cucumber　　　きゅうり
kyūri

curtain　　　カーテン
kāten

(to) dance　おどる
odoru

dandelion　タンポポ
tanpopo

date　ひづけ
hizuke

deer　しか
shika

desert　さばく
sabaku

desk　つくえ
tsukue

dirty　きたない
kitanai

Dd

dog

いぬ
inu

doghouse

いぬごや
inugoya

doll

にんぎょう
ningyō

dollhouse

にんぎょうのいえ
ningyō-no ie

dolphin

イルカ
iruka

donkey

ろば
roba

dragon

りゅう
ryū

dragonfly　　とんぼ
tonbo

(to) draw　　えをかく
e-o kaku

dress　　ドレス
doresu

(to) drink　　のむ
nomu

drum　　ドラム、たいこ
doramu, taiko

duck　　あひる
ahiru

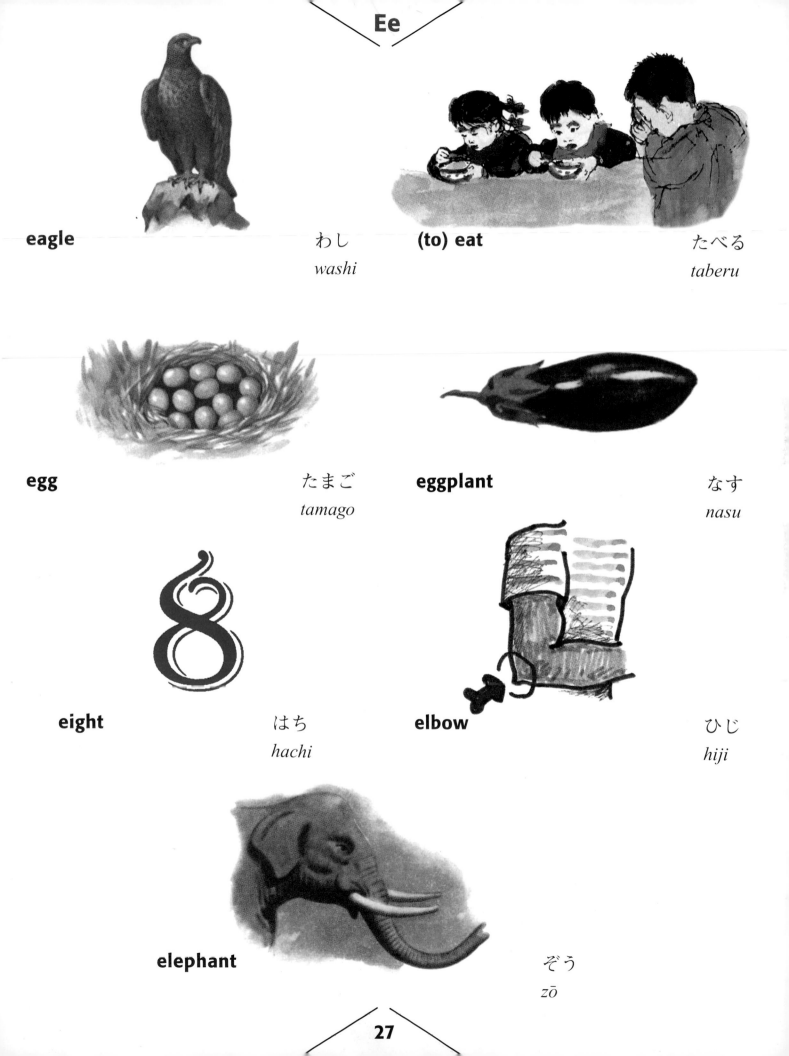

eagle　わし
washi

(to) eat　たべる
taberu

egg　たまご
tamago

eggplant　なす
nasu

eight　はち
hachi

elbow　ひじ
hiji

elephant　ぞう
zō

empty　　　から
kara

engine　　　エンジン
enjin

envelope　　　ふうとう
hūtō

escalator　　　エスカレーター
esukarētā

Eskimo　　　エスキモー
esukimō

(to) explore　　　たんけんする
tanken-suru

eye　　　め
me

face かお
kao

fan せんぷうき
senpūki

father おとうさん
o-tōsan

fear おそれ
osore

feather はね
hane

(to) feed えさをやる
esa-o yaru

fence かこい
kakoi

fern しだ
shida

field のはら
nohara

field mouse のねずみ
nonezumi

finger ゆび
yubi

fir tree えぞまつ
ezomatsu

fire　　　　ひ
hi

fish　　　　さかな
sakana

(to) fish　　　　つる
tsuru

fist　　　　こぶし
kobushi

five　　　　ご
go

flag　　　　はた
hata

flashlight　かいちゅうでんとう
kaichūdentō

(to) float　ただよう
tadayou

flower　はな
hana

(to) fly　とぶ
tobu

foot　あし
ashi

fork　フォーク
fōku

fountain　ふんすい
hunsui

four よん、し
yon, shi

fox きつね
kitsune

frame がくぶち
gakubuchi

friend ともだち
tomodachi

frog かえる
kaeru

fruit くだもの
kudamono

furniture かぐ
kagu

garden にわ
niwa

gate ゲート、もん
gēto, mon

(to) gather あつめる
atsumeru

geranium ゼラニウム
zeranyūmu

giraffe きりん
kirin

girl おんなのこ
onna-noko

(to) give あげる
ageru

glass グラス
gurasu

glasses めがね
megane

globe ちきゅうぎ
chikyūgi

glove てぶくろ
tebukuro

goat やぎ
yagi

goldfish   きんぎょ
kingyo

"Good Night"   おやすみなさい
o-yasumi-nasai

"Good-bye"   さようなら
sayōnara

goose   がちょう
gatyō

grandfather   そふ、おじいさん
sohu, o-jiisan

grandmother   そぼ、おばあさん
sobo, o-bāsan

grapes

ぶどう
budō

grasshopper

きりぎりす
kirigirisu

green

みどり
midori

greenhouse

おんしつ
onshitsu

guitar

ギター
gitā

Hh

hammer かなずち
kanazuchi

hammock ハンモック
hanmokku

hamster ハムスター
hamusutā

hand て
te

handbag ハンドバッグ
handobaggu

handkerchief ハンカチ
hankachi

harvest　とりいれ
toriire

hat　ぼうし
bōshi

hay　ほしくさ
hoshikusa

headdress　あたまかざり
atamakazari

heart　こころ
kokoro

hedgehog　はりねずみ
harinezumi

hen めんどり
mendori

(to) hide かくれる
kakureru

highway ハイウェイ
haiwei

honey はちみつ
hachimitsu

horns つの
tsuno

horse うま
uma

horseshoe   ていてつ
teitetsu

hourglass   すなどけい
sunadokei

house   いえ
ie

(to) hug   だく
daku

hydrant   しょうかせん
shōkasen

ice cream　アイスクリーム
aisukurīmu

ice cubes　こおり
kōri

ice-skating　アイススケート
aisusukēto

instrument　がっき
gakki

iris　しょうぶ
shōbu

iron　アイロン
airon

island　しま
shima

jacket　　　　うわぎ
uwagi

jam　　　　ジャム
jamu

jigsaw puzzle　　　ジグゾーパズル
jiguzō-pazuru

jockey　　　　ジョッキー、きし
jokkī, kishi

juggler　　　きょくげいし
kyokugeishi

(to) jump　　　とびこえる
tobikoeru

kangaroo　カンガルー
kangarū

key　かぎ
kagi

kitten　こねこ
koneko

knife　ナイフ
naifu

knight　きし
kishi

(to) knit　あむ
amu

knot　むすびめ
musubime

koala bear　コアラ
koara

ladder

はしご
hashigo

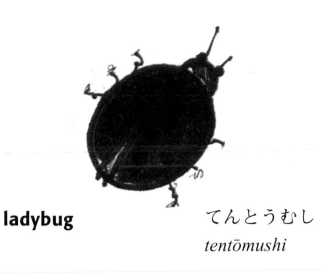

ladybug

てんとうむし
tentōmushi

lamb

こひつじ
kohitsuji

lamp

ランプ
ranpu

(to) lap

なめる
nameru

laughter

わらい
warai

lavender　ラベンダー
rabendā

lawn mower　しばかりき
shibakariki

leaf　は
ha

leg　あし
ashi

lemon　レモン
remon

lettuce　レタス
retasu

lightbulb
でんきゅう
denkyū

lighthouse
とうだい
tōdai

lilac
ライラック、むらさき
rairakku, murasaki

lion
ライオン
raion

(to) listen
きく
kiku

lobster
いせえび、ロブスター
iseebi, robusutā

lock

じょう

jō

lovebird

ボタンインコ

botan-inko

luggage

にもつ

nimotsu

lumberjack

きこり

kikori

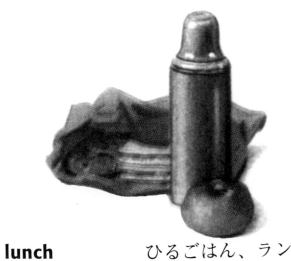

lunch

ひるごはん、ランチ

hirugohan, ranchi

lynx

おおやまねこ

ōyamaneko

magazine ざっし
zasshi

magician てじなし
tejinashi

magnet じしゃく
jishaku

map ちず
chizu

maple leaf もみじ
momiji

marketplace いちば
ichiba

mask マスク、おめん
masuku, o-men

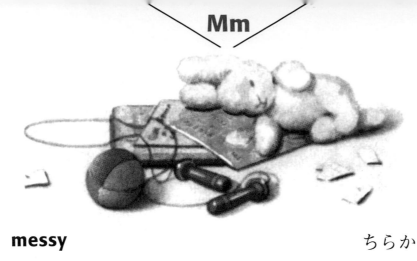

messy

ちらかした
chirakashita

milkman

ぎゅうにゅうや
gyūnyūya

mirror

かがみ
kagami

mitten

ミトン
miton

money

おかね
o-kane

monkey

さる
saru

moon

つき
tsuki

mother おかあさん
o-kāsan

mountain やま
yama

mouse ねずみ
nezumi

mouth くち
kuchi

mushroom きのこ
kinoko

music おんがく
ongaku

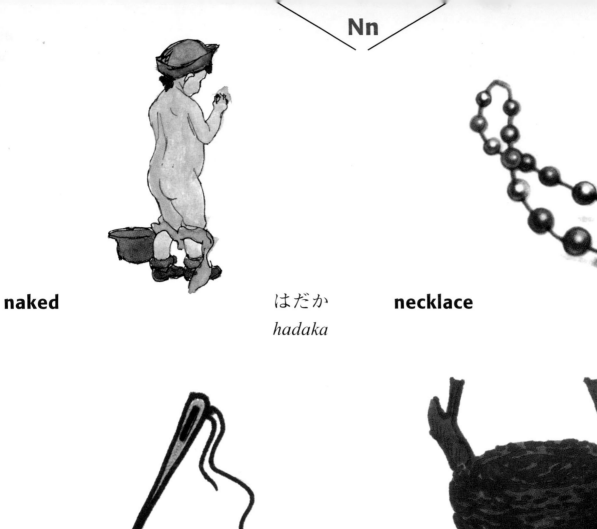

naked

はだか

hadaka

necklace

ネックレス

nekkuresu

needle

はり

hari

nest

す

su

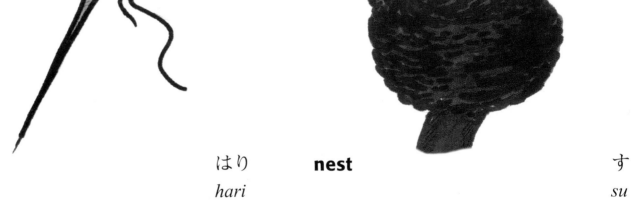

newspaper

しんぶん

shinbun

nightingale　うぐいす
uguisu

nine　く、きゅう
ku, kyū

notebook　ノート
noto

number　すうじ
sūji

nut　このみ
konomi

oar

オール
ōru

ocean liner

きせん
kisen

old

としとった
toshitotta

one

いち
ichi

onion

たまねぎ
tamanegi

open ひらいた
hiraita

orange オレンジ
orenji

ostrich だちょう
dachō

owl ふくろう
hukurō

ox おうし
oushi

padlock　なんきんじょう
nankinjō

paint　えのぐ
enogu

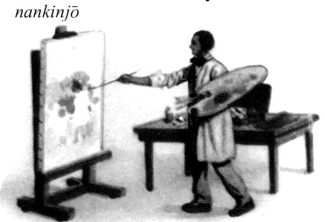

painter

がか
gaka

pajamas　パジャマ
pajama

palm tree　しゅろ、やし
shuro, yashi

paper　かみ
kami

parachute　パラシュート
parashūto

park　こうえん
kōen

parrot　おおむ
ōmu

passport　パスポート、りょけん
pasupōto, ryoken

patch　つぎ
tsugi

path　こみち
komichi

peach　もも
momo

pear　なし
nashi

pebble

こいし
koishi

(to) peck

ついばむ
tsuibamu

(to) peel

かわをむく
kawa-o muku

pelican

ペリカン
perikan

pencil

えんぴつ
enpitsu

penguin

ペンギン
pengin

people

ひとびと
hitobito

piano ピアノ
piano

pickle すずけのきゅうり、ピクルス
suzuke-no kyūri, pikurusu

pie パイ
pai

pig ぶた
buta

pigeon はと
hato

pillow まくら
makura

pin ピン
pin

pine

まつ
matsu

pineapple

パイナップル
painappuru

pit

たね
tane

pitcher

みずさし
mizusashi

plate

さら
sara

platypus

かものはし
kamonohashi

(to) play　　　あそぶ
asobu

plum　　　プラム、スモモ
puramu, sumomo

polar bear　　　しろくま
shirokuma

pony　　　ポニー
ponī

pot　　　なべ
nabe

potato　　　ポテト
poteto

(to) pour つぐ
tsugu

present おくりもの、プレゼント
okurimono, purezento

(to) pull ひく
hiku

pumpkin かぼちゃ
kabocha

Qq

puppy こいぬ
koinu

queen じょうおう
jōō

rabbit　　　うさぎ
usagi

raccoon　　　あらいぐま
araiguma

racket　　　ラケット
raketto

radio　　　ラジオ
rajio

radish　　　はつかだいこん
hatsuka daikon

raft　　いかだ
ikada

rain　　あめ
ame

rainbow　　にじ
niji

raincoat　レインコート
reinkōto

raspberry　きいちご
kiichigo

(to) read　　　　よむ
yomu

red　　　あか
aka

refrigerator　　れいぞうこ
reizōko

rhinoceros　　さい
sai

ring　　ゆびわ
yubiwa

(to) ring   ベルをならす
beru-o narasu

river   かわ
kawa

road   みち
michi

rocket   ロケット
roketto

roof   やね
yane

rooster   おんどり
ondori

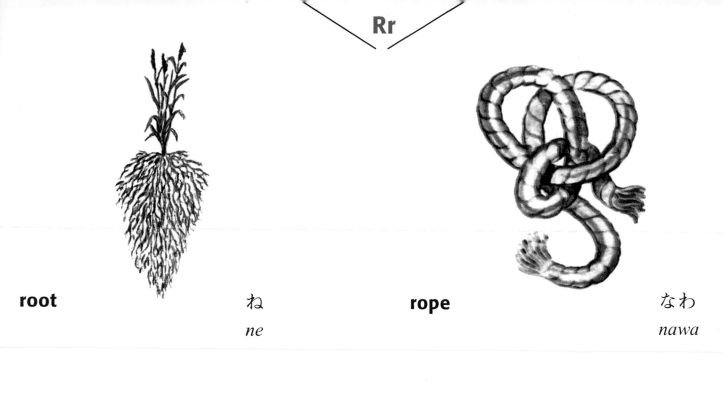

root　ね
ne

rope　なわ
nawa

rose　ばら
bara

(to) row　こぐ
kogu

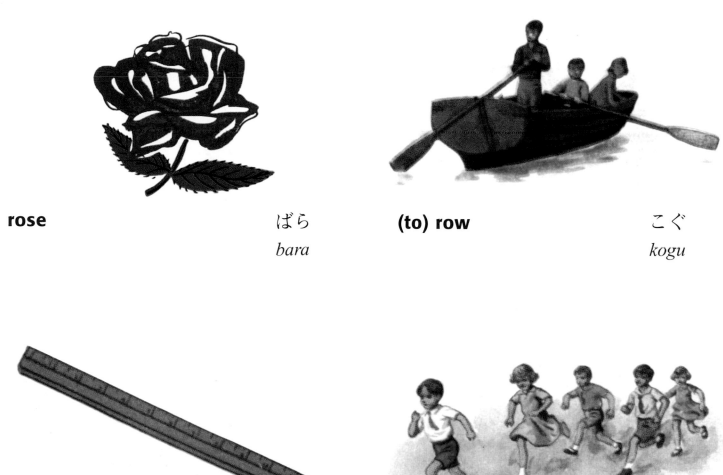

ruler　じょうぎ
jōgi

(to) run　はしる
hashiru

safety pin　　あんぜんピン
anzenpin

(to) sail　　こうこうする
kōkō-suru

sailor　　すいへい
suihei

salt　　しお
shio

scarf　　えりまき
erimaki

school　　がっこう
gakkō

scissors

はさみ
hasami

screwdriver

ねじまわし
nejimawashi

seagull

かもめ
kamome

seesaw

シーソー
shīsō

seven

なな、しち
nana, shichi

(to) sew

ぬう
nuu

shark　　　さめ
same

sheep　　　ひつじ
hitsuji

shell　　　かい
kai

shepherd　　　ひつじかい
hitsujikai

ship　　　ふね
hune

shirt　　　シャツ
shatsu

shoe くつ
kutsu

shovel シャベル
shaberu

(to) show みせる
miseru

shower シャワー
shawā

shutter よろいど
yoroido

sick びょうき
byōki

sieve　ふるい
hurui

(to) sing　うたう
utau

(to) sit　すわる
suwaru

six　ろく
roku

sled　そり
sori

(to) sleep　ねむる
nemuru

small ちいさい
chiisai

smile ほほえみ
hohoemi

snail かたつむり
katatsumuri

snake へび
hebi

snow ゆき
yuki

sock ソックス
sokkusu

sofa　　ソファー
sofã

sparrow　　すずめ
suzume

spider　　くも
kumo

spiderweb　　くものす
kumo-no su

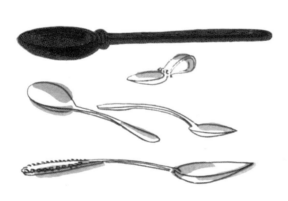

spoon　　スプーン
supūn

squirrel　　リス
risu

stairs かいだん
kaidan

stamp きって
kitte

starfish ヒトデ
hitode

stork コオノトリ
kōnotori

stove ガスだい
gasudai

strawberry いちご
ichigo

subway ちかてつ
chikatetsu

sugar cube かくざとう
kakuzatō

sun たいよう
taiyō

sunflower ひまわり
himawari

sweater セーター
sētā

(to) sweep はく
haku

swing ぶらんこ
buranko

table テーブル
tēburu

teapot きゅうす
kyūsu

teddy bear くまのぬいぐるみ
kuma-no nuigurumi

television テレビ
terebi

10

ten じゅう
jū

tent テント
tento

theater げきじょう
gekijō

thimble ゆびぬき
yubinuki

(to) think かんがえる
kangaeru

three さん
san

tie ネクタイ
nekutai

(to) tie むすぶ
musubu

tiger とら
tora

toaster トースター
tōsutā

tomato トマト
tomato

toucan オオハシ
ōhashi

towel タオル
taoru

tower とう
tō

toy box　おもちゃばこ
omochabako

tracks　レール
rēru

train station　えき
eki

tray　おぼん
o-bon

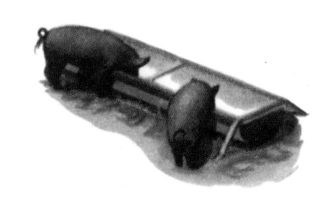

tree　き
ki

trough　かいばおけ
kaibaoke

truck　トラック
torakku

trumpet　トランペット
toranpetto

tulip　チューリップ
chūrippu

tunnel　トンネル
tonneru

turtle　うみがめ
umigame

twins　ふたご
hutago

two　に
ni

umbrella かさ
kasa

uphill のぼりざか
noborizaka

Vv

vase かびん
kabin

veil ベール
bēru

village

むら
mura

violet

すみれ
sumire

violin

バイオリン
baiorin

voyage

ふなたび
hunatabi

waiter

ウェイター
weitā

(to) wake up

めざめる
mezameru

walrus

せいうち
seiuchi

(to) wash

あらう
arau

watch

とけい
tokei

(to) watch

みつめる
mitsumeru

(to) water みずをやる
mizu-o yaru

waterfall たき
taki

watering can じょうろ
jōro

watermelon すいか
suika

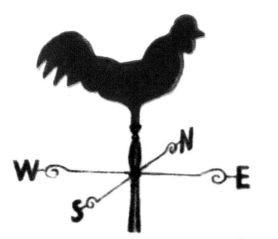

weather vane かざみどり
kazamidori

(to) weigh はかる
hakaru

whale くじら
kujira

wheel しゃりん
sharin

wheelbarrow ておしぐるま
teoshi-guruma

whiskers ほおひげ
hoohige

(to) whisper ささやく
sasayaku

whistle ふえ
hue

Ww

white

しろ
shiro

wig

かつら
katsura

wind

かぜ
kaze

window

まど
mado

wings

つばさ
tsubasa

winter

ふゆ
huyu

wolf

おおかみ
ōkami

wood

まき
maki

word

ことば
kotoba

(to) write

かく
kaku

yellow

きいろ
kiiro

Zz

zebra

しまうま
shimauma

bōshi — hat
botan-inko — lovebird
bōto — boat
budō — grapes
buranko — swing
burashi — brush
buresuretto — bracelet
buta — pig
būtsu — boot
byōki — sick

C

chairo — brown
chiisai — small
chikatetsu — subway
chikyūgi — globe
chīzu — cheese
chizu — map
chirakashita — messy
chō — butterfly
chokorēto — chocolate
chūrippu — tulip

A

āchi — arch
ahiru — duck
ageru — (to) give
airon — iron
aisusukēto — ice-skating
aisukurīmu — ice cream
aka-chan — baby
aka — red
aki — autumn
ame — candy
ame — rain
amu — (to) knit
ani — brother (older)
anzen pin — safety pin
ao — blue
araiguma — raccoon
arau — (to) wash
arufabetto — alphabet
asagohan — breakfast
ashi — foot, leg
asobu — (to) play
atamakazari — headdress
atsumeru — (to) gather

D

dachō — ostrich
daku — (to) hug
denkyū — lightbulb
dōkesh — clown
donburi — bowl
doresu — dress
doramu — drum

E

eda — branch
eki — station
enjin — engine
enogu — paint
enpitsu — pencil
entotsu — chimney
e-o kaku — (to) draw
erimaki — scarf

B

baiorin — violin
baketsu — bucket
banana — banana
bara — rose
basha — coach
beddo — bed
benchi — bench
beru — bell
bēru — veil
beru-o narasu — (to) ring
beruto — belt
bībā — beaver
bin — bottle
bōru — ball

E (esa)

esa-o yaru — (to) feed
esukarētā — escalator
esukimō — Eskimo
ezomatsu — fir tree

F

fōku — fork

G

gachō — goose
gaka — painter
gakki — instrument
gakkō — school
gakubuchi — frame
gekijō — theater
gasudai — stove
gēto — gate
gitā — guitar
go — five
gurasu — glass
gyūnyūya — milkman

H

ha — leaf
hachi — bee
hachi — eight
hachimitsu — honey
hadaka — naked
haiwei — highway
hakaru — (to) weigh
hakobu — (to) carry
haku — (to) sweep
hamusutā — hamster
hana — blossom
hane — feather
handobaggu — handbag
hankachi — handkerchief
hanmokku — hammock

Index

hari	needle
hasami	scissors
hashi	bridge
hashigo	ladder
hashiru	(to) run
hana	flower
harinezumi	hedgehog
hata	flag
hato	pigeon
hatsuka daikon	radish
hau	(to) crawl
hebi	snake
hi	fire
hiji	elbow
hikōki	airplane
hiku	(to) pull
himawari	sunflower
hiraita	open
hirugohan	lunch
hitobito	people
hitode	starfish
hitsuji	sheep
hitsujikai	shepherd
hizuke	date
hohoemi	smile
hōki	broom
hon	book
hone	bone
hoohige	whiskers
horaana	cave
hoshikusa	hay
hue	whistle
hukurō	owl
hunatabi	voyage
hune	ship
hunsui	fountain
hurui	sieve
hūsen	balloon
hutago	twins
hūtō	envelope
huton	comforter
huyu	winter

I

ichi	one
ichiba	market
ichigo	strawberry
ie	house
ikada	raft
inu	dog
inugoya	doghouse
iruka	dolphin
iseebi	lobster
isu	chair

J

jamu	jam
jidōsha	car
jiguzo-pazuru	jigsaw puzzle
jishaku	magnet
jitensha	bicycle
jokkī	jockey
jō	lock
jōgi	ruler
joō	queen
jōro	watering can
jū	ten
jūtan	carpet

K

kabin	vase
kabocha	pumpkin
kabutomushi	beetle
kaeru	frog
kagami	mirror
kago	basket
kagu	furniture
kai	shell
kaibaoke	trough
kaichūdentō	flashlight
kaidan	stairs
kakoi	fence
kaku	(to) write
kakuzatō	sugar cube

kakureru	(to) hide
kamera	camera
kami	paper
kamome	seagull
kamonohashi	platypus
kamoshika	antelope
kanazuchi	hammer
kangaeru	(to) think
kangarū	kangaroo
kanmuri	crown
kanū	canoe
kao	face
kāpetto	carpet
kara	empty
kasa	umbrella
katatsumuri	snail
kāten	curtain
katsura	wig
kawa	river
kawa-o muku	(to) peel
kazamidori	weather vane
kaze	wind
keijiban	bulletin board
kēki	cake
ki	tree
kiichigo	raspberry
kiiro	yellow
kikori	lumberjack
kiku	listen
kinoko	mushroom
kingyo	goldfish
kirigirisu	grasshopper
kirin	giraffe
kisen	ocean liner
kissaten	café
kishi	knight, jockey
kitanai	dirty
kitsune	fox
kitte	stamp
koara	koala bear
kobushi	fist
kōen	park

kogu	(to) row
kohitsuji	lamb
koinu	puppy
koishi	pebble
kokoro	heart
kōkō-suru	(to) sail
kōnotori	stork
komichi	path
kōmori	bat
koneko	kitten
konomi	nut
kōri	ice cubes
koruku	cork
kōto	coat
kotoba	word
ku	nine
kuchi	mouth
kudamono	fruit
kujira	whale
kuma	bear
kuma-no nuigurumi	teddy bear
kumo	cloud
kumo	spider
kumo-no su	spiderweb
kurakkā	cracker
kurisumasu tsurī	Christmas tree
kuro	black
kushi	comb
kutsu	shoe
kyabetsu	cabbage
kyappu	cap
kyaputen	captain
kyokugeishi	juggler
kyū	nine
kyūri	cucumber
kyūsu	teapot

M

mado	window
maki	wood
makura	pillow
maruhanabachi	bumblebee
masuku	mask
matsu	pine
me	eye
megane	glasses

mendori	hen
meushi	cow
mezameru	(to) wake up
michi	road
midori	green
miseru	(to) show
miton	mitten
mitsumeru	(to) watch
mizu-o yaru	(to) water
mizusashi	pitcher
momiji	maple leaf
momo	peach
mon	gate
mura	village
murasaki	lilac
musubime	knot

N

nabe	pot
naifu	knife
naku	(to) cry
nameru	(to) lap
nana	seven
nankinjō	padlock
nashi	pear
nasu	eggplant
nawa	rope
ne	root
nejimawashi	screwdriver
nekkuresu	necklace
neko	cat
nekutai	tie
nemuru	(to) sleep
nezumi	mouse
ni	two
niji	rainbow
nimotsu	luggage
ningyō	doll
ningyō-no ie	dollhouse
ninjin	carrot
niwa	garden
noborizaka	uphill
noboru	(to) climb
nohara	field

nomu	(to) drink
nonezumi	field mouse
nōto	notebook
nuu	(to) sew

O

o-bāsan	grandmother
o-bon	tray
odoru	(to) dance
ōhashi	toucan
o-jiisan	grandfather
ōkami	wolf
o-kane	money
o-kāsan	mother
okurimono	present
o-men	mask
ōmu	parrot
ōmugi	barley
omochabako	toy box
ondori	rooster
ongaku	music
onna-no ko	girl
onshitsu	greenhouse
ooyamaneko	lynx
orenji	orange
ōru	oar
osore	fear
otoko-no ko	boy
otōto	brother (younger)
o-tōsan	father
oushi	ox
o-yasumi-nasai	"Good Night"

P

pai	pie
painappuru	pineapple
pan	bread
panya	baker
parashūto	parachute
pasupōto	passport
pajama	pajamas
pengin	penguin
perikan	pelican
piano	piano
pikurusu	pickle
pin	pin
ponī	pony
poteto	potato
puramu	plum
purezento	present

R

rabendā	lavender
rairakku	lilac
raion	lion
rajio	radio
raketto	racket
rakuda	camel
ranchi	lunch
ranpu	lamp
rashinban	compass
reinkōto	raincoat
reizōko	refrigerator
remon	lemon
rēru	tracks
retasu	lettuce
ringo	apple
risu	squirrel
roba	donkey
robusutā	lobster
roketto	rocket
roku	six
rōsoku	candle
ryōken	passport
ryōri-suru	(to) cook
ryū	dragon
ryukkusakku	backpack

S

sabaku	desert
saboten	cactus
sai	rhinoceros
sākasu	circus
sakuranbo	cherry
same	shark
san	tree
sara	plate
saru	monkey
sasayaku	(to) whisper
satō	sugar
sayōnara	"Good-bye"
seiuchi	walrus
senchō	captain
senpūki	fan
sētā	sweater
shaberu	shovel
sharin	wheel
shatsu	shirt
shawā	shower
shi	four
shibakariki	lawn mower
shichi	seven
shida	fern
shīsō	seesaw
shika	deer
shika-no tsuno	antlers
shima	island
shimauma	zebra
shinbun	newspaper
shio	salt
shiro	castle
shiro	white
shirokuma	polar bear
shōbu	iris
shōkasen	hydrant

shuro	palm tree
sobo	grandmother
sofā	sofa
sohu	grandfather
sōgankyō	binoculars
sokkusu	sock
sori	sled
su	nest
suihei	sailor
suika	watermelon
suisō	aquarium
sūji	number
sumire	violet
sumomo	plum
sunadokei	hourglass
sunahama	beach
supūn	spoon
suzume	sparrow
suwaru	(to) sit
suzuke-no kyūri	pickle

T

taberu	(to) eat
tadayou	(to) float
taiko	drum
taiyō	sun
taki	waterfall
takushī	cab
tamago	egg
tamanegi	onion
tane	pit
tanken-suru	(to) explore
tanpopo	dandelion
tanuki	badger
taoru	towel
taru	barrel
te	hand
tebukuro	glove
tēburu	table
teitetsu	horseshoe
tejinashi	magician
tento	tent
tentōmushi	ladybug

teoshi-guruma	wheelbarrow
terebi	television
tō	tower
tobikoeru	(to) jump
tobu	(to) fly
tōdai	lighthouse
tokei	watch
tomato	tomato
tomodaci	friend
tōmorokoshi	corn
tonbo	dragonfly
tonneru	tunnel
tora	tiger
torakku	truck
toranpetto	trumpet
toranpu	card
tori	bird
toriire	harvest
torikago	birdcage
toshitotta	old
tōsutā	toaster
tsugi	patch
tsugu	(to) pour
tsuibamu	(to) peck
tsubasa	wings
tsuki	moon
tsukue	desk
tsumiki	blocks
tsuno	horns
tsuru	(to) fish

U

uguisu	nightingale
uma	horse
umigame	turtle
usagi	rabbit
utau	(to) sing
uwagi	jacket

W

wani	alligator
warai	laughter
washi	eagle
weitā	waiter

Y

ya	arrow
yagi	goat
yokogiru	(to) cross
yama	mountain
yane	roof
yashi	palm tree
yashi-no mi	coconut
yomu	(to) read
yon	four
yoroido	shutter
yubi	finger
yubinuki	thimble
yubiwa	ring
yuki	snow
yurikago	cradle

Z

zasshi	magazine
zeranyūmu	geranium
zō	elephant

Folk Tales from Bohemia
Adolf Wenig

This folk tale collection is one of a kind, focusing uniquely on humankind's struggle with evil in the world. Delicately ornate red and black text and illustrations set the mood.

Ages 9 and up

90 pages • red and black illustrations • 5 1/2 x 8 1/4 • 0-7818-0718-2 • W • $14.95hc • (786)

Czech, Moravian and Slovak Fairy Tales
Parker Fillmore

Fifteen different classic, regional folk tales and 23 charming illustrations whisk the reader to places of romance, deception, royalty, and magic.

Ages 12 and up

243 pages • 23 b/w illustrations • 5 1/2 x 8 1/4 • 0-7818-0714-X • W • $14.95 hc • (792)

Glass Mountain: Twenty-Eight Ancient Polish Folk Tales and Fables
W.S. Kuniczak

Illustrated by Pat Bargielski

As a child in a far-away misty corner of Volhynia, W.S. Kuniczak was carried away to an extraordinary world of magic and illusion by the folk tales of his Polish nurse.

171 pages • 6 x 9 • 8 illustrations • 0-7818-0552-X • W • $16.95hc • (645)

Old Polish Legends
Retold by F.C. Anstruther

Wood engravings by J. Sekalski

This fine collection of eleven fairy tales, with an introduction by Zymunt Nowakowski, was first published in Scotland during World War II.

66 pages • 7 1/4 x 9 • 11 woodcut engravings • 0-7818-0521-X • W • $11.95hc • (653)

Folk Tales from Russia
by Donald A. Mackenzie

With nearly 200 pages and 8 full-page black-and-white illustrations, the reader will be charmed by these legendary folk tales that symbolically weave magical fantasy with the historic events of Russia's past.

Ages 12 and up

192 pages • 8 b/w illustrations • 5 1/2 x 8 1/4 • 0-7818-0696-8 • W • $12.50hc • (788)

Fairy Gold: A Book of Classic English Fairy Tales
Chosen by Ernest Rhys

Illustrated by Herbert Cole

Forty-nine imaginative black and white illustrations accompany thirty classic tales, including such beloved stories as "Jack and the Bean Stalk" and "The Three Bears."

Ages 12 and up

236 pages • 5 1/2 x 8 1/4 • 49 b/w illustrations • 0-7818-0700-X • W • $14.95hc • (790)

Tales of Languedoc: From the South of France
Samuel Jacques Brun
For readers of all ages, here is a masterful collection of folk tales from the south of France.
Ages 12 and up
248 pages • 33 b/w sketches • 5 1/2 x 8 1/4 • 0-7818-0715-8 • W • $14.95hc • (793)

Twenty Scottish Tales and Legends
Edited by Cyril Swinson
Illustrated by Allan Stewart
Twenty enchanting stories take the reader to an extraordinary world of magic harps, angry giants, mysterious spells and gallant Knights.
Ages 9 and up
215 pages • 5 1/2 x 8 1/4 • 8 b/w illustrations • 0-7818-0701-8 • W • $14.95 hc • (789)

Swedish Fairy Tales
Translated by H. L. Braekstad
A unique blending of enchantment, adventure, comedy, and romance make this collection of Swedish fairy tales a must-have for any library.
Ages 9 and up
190 pages • 21 b/w illustrations • 51/2 x 81/4 • 0-7818-0717-4 • W • $12.50hc • (787)

The Little Mermaid and Other Tales
Hans Christian Andersen
Here is a near replica of the first American edition of 27 classic fairy tales from the masterful Hans Christian Andersen.
Ages 9 and up
508 pages • b/w illustrations • 6 x 9 • 0-7818-0720-4 • W • $19.95hc • (791)

Pakistani Folk Tales: Toontoony Pie and Other Stories
Ashraf Siddiqui and Marilyn Lerch
Illustrated by Jan Fairservis
In these 22 folk tales are found not only the familiar figures of folklore—kings and beautiful princesses—but the magic of the Far East, cunning jackals, and wise holy men.
Ages 7 and up
158 pages • 6 1/2 x 8 1/2 • 38 illustrations • 0-7818-0703-4 • W • $12.50hc • (784)

Folk Tales from Chile
Brenda Hughes
This selection of 15 tales gives a taste of the variety of Chile's rich folklore. Fifteen charming illustrations accompany the text.
Ages 7 and up
121 pages • 5 1/2 x 8 1/4 • 15 illustrations • 0-7818-0712-3 • W • $12.50hc • (785)

All prices subject to change. **To purchase Hippocrene Books** contact your local bookstore, call (718) 454-2366, or write to: HIPPOCRENE BOOKS, 171 Madison Avenue, New York, NY 10016. Please enclose check or money order, adding $5.00 shipping (UPS) for the first book and $.50 for each additional book.